KISSing Golf

The Keep It Simple (Stupid) Instructional Method

Mark Shatz, Ph.D.

Illustrated by Roger Drake

CHICAGO SPECTRUM PRESS
EVANSTON, IL 60201

CHICAGO SPECTRUM PRESS
1571 SHERMAN AVENUE
EVANSTON, IL 60201
1-800-594-5190

Printed in Canada

10 9 8 7 6 5 4 3 2 1

ISBN: 1-886094-59-4

Cover design by Dorothy Kavka

Dedication

To the beginning golfers who accept the challenge to carry on the tradition of this great game.

Acknowledgments

The birth of this book was nurtured by the love and support of my friends and family. I thank you all.

Special thanks are extended to the following individuals who contributed to the development of *KISSing Golf*:

* Roger Drake for his wonderful illustrations.

* Golf professionals Kelly Morrow, Mike Durant, and Ned Weaver for their technical advice.

* Amy Coombs, Debby Johnston, Mike Nern, J. T. Schneider, Amanda Carroll, Billie Mautz, Kathy Shepherd, and Jay Shatz for their editorial comments.

* Steve Evec, Kelly Morrow, and the staff at Eaglesticks Golf Course for allowing me to contribute to their program. (If you are ever in Southeastern Ohio, take the time to play one of the finest public golf courses in the country.)

* Alex, for his many barks of approval, will get an extra large can of dog food.

Table of Contents

Chapter One
Overview

Golf is the most over-taught and least-learned human endeavor. If they taught sex the way they teach golf, the race would have died out years ago.

-Jim Murray

What do golf and sex have in common? First of all, both are popular recreational pastimes that provide moderate exercise. Next, golf and sex are more fun when played with someone else and each can be enjoyed without being very good at it. Finally, men often lie about their performance.

An introduction to golf, like a first kiss, should be simple and enjoyable. For many first-time golfers, the complexity of traditional golf teaching methods takes the fun out of learning how to golf. Beginning golfers do not need, nor do they desire, to have their minds cluttered with technical information. What they want is a simple and easy way to learn to play golf. So simple that anyone can become a golfer and so easy that everyone will enjoy learning the game. To the rescue comes a revolutionary training program, *KISSing Golf: The Keep it Simple (Stupid) Instructional Method.*

What is the KISSing Golf *Approach?*

KISSing Golf is a golf "starter" manual that addresses only the specific needs of beginners. This book is for golfers who previously avoided the game because it was too frustrating, have limited time to practice, and intend to pursue golf as a part-time endeavor.

I drew on my training and experience as an educational psychologist and golf instructor to develop a program that can be completed quickly and is based on sound instructional principles. The various *KISSing Golf* training exercises are integrated into a self-paced instructional program that will teach you how to play golf in a step-by-step manner. The program can readily be used by golfers of different ages and athletic abilities.

Learning, in any form, should be enjoyable. Too often, individuals are so focused on results that the pleasure of learning is lost. I have created a program that is fun to complete and a book that is enjoyable to read. After all, golf is just a game and as a game it should be pleasurable.

Does the KISSing Golf *Method Work?*

Yes! To make sure this program lives up to its promises—simple, easy, and fun—the *KISSing Golf* method has been thoroughly evaluated. Novice golfers have tried the instructional program and I used their feedback to refine and improve the program. This field testing assures that the *KISSing Golf* method works.

How is KISSing Golf *Unique?*

KISSing Golf differs in content and style from other golf books. In addition to teaching the fundamentals of golf, *KISSing Golf* uses a variety of instructional and psychological features to raise your golf IQ and maximize your enjoyment of the game. Your "guides" into the world of golf are the following three characters:

The Mechanic

How do I hold the club? Why can't I hit the ball? Why did I just hit my spouse with the ball? If you want answers to swing-related questions, just ask the Mechanic.

Ms. Etiquette

Golf is a game with a set of well defined rules and a tradition of "proper" behavior. Ms. Etiquette will teach you the rules and etiquette of golf and help you avoid making a golfing faux pas.

The Golf Guy

The Golf Guy will fill your head with golf trivia and help you talk, think, and act like a proverbial golfer. As a philosopher once said, "It is better, of course, to know useless things than to know nothing."

The following features supplement the instruction.

• Skill ✔ list

A summary of the key instructional concepts are provided in the Skill ✔ list.

• Practice Tips

Additional instructional suggestions and practice guidelines are described in the Practice Tips section.

• Training Center

The Training Center contains the structured practice drills that you will use to develop and refine your golfing skills. The self-paced program allows you to determine the rate at which you learn how to golf.

• *Repair Shop*

You will admit yourself to the Repair Shop when your swing breaks down. Describe your problems to the Mechanic and he will help you repair your swing.

• *Reward*

As with any complex skill, it takes time and practice to become a golfer. To keep you working toward your goals, some form of reward must be available for your hard work. In the Reward section, golf-related rewards are proposed for the completion of each chapter.

Is KISSing Golf for You?

If you want to learn how to golf so you can enjoy the game and play with others, then this book is for you. The *KISSing Golf* method will simply and effectively teach you the skills you need to play a round of golf without completely embarrassing yourself. Will you be a great golfer? No! You will, however, be able to go out and enjoy the game. If you aspire to continue with golf, the fundamental skills taught by the *KISSing Golf* program can be easily fine-tuned.

How Do I Use This Book?

There are two ways to use this book. First, use it as a self-paced instructional program; you read the book and complete the activities on your own and at your own rate. This book can also be used by an experienced golfer to teach a family member or friend how to golf. As a teacher you would read the book, use the *KISSing Golf* instructional strategies to teach the skills, and assign the Training Center exercises. If you adhere to the instructional program, your student will achieve the same degree of success as someone who follows the self-paced program.

What Equipment Do I Need?

Golfers spend several billion dollars annually on equipment. Do you need to contribute to that outrageous sum? No! To use the total *KISSing Golf* program you only need the following equipment: putter, three-wood or five-wood, nine-iron or pitching wedge, seven-iron, five-iron, three golf balls, and three tennis balls. When you complete the *KISSing Golf* program you will be ready to play a round of golf. After that, you will probably want to acquire additional equipment.

To start the program, you will only need a putter, three golf balls, and three tennis balls. After you collect those items, proceed to Chapter Two.

Chapter Two
Putting: Indoors

The best way to putt is the way you putt.

—Golf proverb

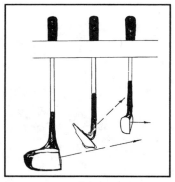

Driver, wedge, and putter

The objective of golf is to take the fewest number of strokes to hit the ball into the hole. To achieve that goal, golfers are allowed to carry and use fourteen different clubs. Although all the clubs might be used in a typical eighteen-hole round of golf, some are used more frequently than others. The three most important golf clubs are the putter, wedge, and driver.

The *KiSSing Golf* method begins with the putter for several reasons. First, as the most frequently used club, the putter is the most important club. As a beginner golfer you may use the putter for approximately 40% of all your shots. Second, the putting stroke is the easiest golf swing to learn. And finally, you can practice putting in the privacy of your home.

Putter

For this chapter, you will need an indoor practice area. A non-shag carpet that is approximately ten feet or longer is ideal. If you do not have such an area, you should purchase an inexpensive indoor putting surface (available at most golf shops).

The Mechanic

The mechanics of putting are individualized. That is, there is no standard or "correct" way to putt. You can use any style that feels comfortable and works. There are, however, some basic techniques that can improve your putting. Let's ask the Mechanic to explain the fundamentals of putting. Experiment with the putter as you read this section.

• *How do I hold the putter?*

Grasp the putter with your left hand approximately one inch below the top of the rubber grip. Place your right hand below your left hand and make sure the thumbs of both hands are pointing straight down the shaft. The palms of both hands should face each other.

Please note that golf is a discriminating sport. Most golf books, equipment, and courses are designed for right-handed players. If you are a lefty, you will have to reverse the instructions to fit your needs.

To help your hands work as a unit you will use either an overlapping or an interlocking grip. For the overlapping grip, the right pinkie finger rests on the groove between the left index finger and left middle finger. For the interlocking grip, the left index finger is crossed over the

Overlapping grip

7

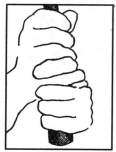

Interlocking grip

Baseball grip

right pinkie finger. Try both the interlocking and overlapping grips and select the grip style that feels most comfortable to you. The interlocking or overlapping grips will initially feel awkward, but will help your hands work as one unit.

If you are unable to use an interlocking or overlapping grip, then you can try a baseball grip. Place all ten fingers on the club with the left index finger and right pinkie finger touching each other.

A critical aspect of the grip is the amount of pressure you apply to hold the club. The proper grip pressure is light yet firm. To determine the proper pressure, try the following. Grip the club as tightly as possible and assign a grip pressure rating of five to your "death" grip. Now hold the club so lightly that the putter is about to fall out of your hands and assign a grip pressure rating of one to your "weakling" grip. The proper grip pressure for putting should fall between a rating of two and three.

• *How do I aim?*

There are two major components of alignment. First, the club must be aimed, or aligned, toward the target. After you grip the club, place the putter directly behind the ball and aim the club at the target, using the alignment mark (e.g., white line) on the top of the putter clubhead. The second major alignment consideration is the position of your body relative to the ball. Your body should be aligned to the left of the target and parallel to the target line.

• *How do I stand?*

To determine the proper stance you will need a piece of notebook-sized paper (8.5 x 11 inches). Along the long side of the paper make the following markings: "A" in the left-hand corner, "B" in the middle, and "C" in the right-hand corner. This paper will be used to identify foot and ball position throughout the book.

Place the paper on the floor and place your feet around the edges (positions "A" and "C"). The distance between the insides of your feet should be approximately 12-16 inches, or shoulder-width apart. Make sure your toes are even with the edges of the paper.

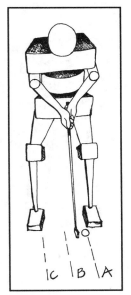

Stance

After your feet are properly set, you will need to identify the proper posture. The first step is to slightly bend your knees. The purpose of the knee flex is to establish an athletic posture that promotes balance. With the proper grip and knee position, hold the putter in front of you at shoulder height. Slowly bend at the waist until the putter hits the floor or ground. You now should be properly aligned and positioned.

The three possible ball positions are noted on the piece of notebook paper that you used to determine foot position. For putting, the ball can be located anywhere between ball positions A and B. That means the ball can be positioned between the middle of the stance and the insole of the left foot.

• *How do I swing?*

The length and speed of the putting stroke are individual preferences. Some players have a long, flowing putting stroke while others use a short, tapping stroke. The most critical aspects of the swing are keeping the

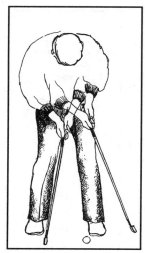

Putting stroke

body still during the stroke and accelerating through the ball. An easy way to assure that you have the proper stroke is to make sure your forward swing is as long or longer than your backswing.

• *How do I remember what to do?*

The Mechanic reminds you that golf is a GASS and you must have enough GASS to play. What does GASS stand for? Grip, Alignment of the club and body, Stance, and Swing—all the elements of the swing routine that will be used for putting and other shots.

Practice Tips: Developing Distance Control

When you shoot a basket, what do you look at? When you throw a baseball, where do you look? When you toss a dart, where do you aim? The answer is the target.

Golf is one of the few sports in which you are taught not to look at a target when performing the activity. Yet, looking at the golf ball during the swing significantly increases the odds of becoming focused on the process of hitting the ball rather than the more important objective of reaching the target. The result is a loss of accuracy.

One of the special training features of the *KiSSing Golf* method is to look at the target while putting the ball. You will discover that this practice technique will help you develop a feel for distance control.

☞ *Stop: Try This*

You probably question your ability to hit a ball without looking at it. To prove that it can be done you should

10

Putting ✔ List

Grip

❑ Place the left hand one inch below the top of the shaft.

❑ Point the thumbs straight down the shaft and palms facing each other.

❑ Use an interlocking, overlapping, or baseball grip.

❑ Maintain constant grip pressure (between levels two and three).

Alignment

❑ Aim the putter at the target.

❑ Align the body parallel to the target.

Stance

❑ Stand with the feet shoulder-width apart.

❑ Position the ball between the feet (ball position A to B).

❑ Bend the knees.

❑ Stand with the back curved and relaxed.

Swing

❑ Use a consistent and repeatable stroke.

❑ Accelerate the club toward the target.

try using a tennis ball in place of the golf ball. Place a shoe or similar sized object on the floor approximately ten feet away. Use the putter to putt the tennis ball to the shoe while looking at the tennis ball. Try again, but this time look at the target (i.e., shoe) while you hit. This first attempt may feel awkward, but with practice you will find that you are a probably a better putter when you look at the target.

Training Center

The training sessions begin with putting the tennis ball to a target. After you acquire the skill of hitting the tennis ball without looking at it, practice putting with a golf ball. Again, begin with short putts and gradually progress to long putts. It will be helpful to alternate putting while looking at the target and at the golf ball.

To progress from one skill level to the next, you must satisfy the performance criteria for that specific skill. For example, the first putting skill is hitting a tennis ball to a target from three feet away while looking at the target. You will continue practicing that skill until you satisfy the performance criteria of three successful putts out of three attempts. Once you have accomplished that skill, you will move to the next level.

The *KISSing Golf* method assures that the initial skills you practice are easily achieved. At times you may feel that a skill is too simple and decide to skip that step. It is crucial that you do not skip any skill level. The final goal of achieving a golf swing is so difficult that you must frequently reward the learning of the fundamentals. Complete each step of the Training Center assignments and keep a record of your performance.

Training Center

Equipment Needed
- *Putter*
- *Three golf balls*
- *Three tennis balls*

Task	Distance	Competence
❏ Hit tennis ball to shoe while looking at shoe	3 feet	3 for 3
❏ Hit golf ball to shoe while looking at shoe	3 feet	3 for 3
❏ Hit tennis ball to shoe while 6 feet looking at shoe	6 feet 9 feet	2 for 3 1 for 3
❏ Hit golf ball to shoe while looking at shoe	6 feet	1 for 3
❏ Hit golf ball to shoe while looking at golf ball	3 feet 6 feet 9 feet	3 for 3 2 for 3 1 for 3

Repair Shop

The Repair Shop is where you go to fix the flaws with your technique. The Mechanic forewarns you that there are usually three types of reactions to his repair suggestions. First, the repairs will immediately fix the problem and the Mechanic will be referred to as a "miracle worker." Second, the swing problem will initially worsen but improve with practice, and the Mechanic becomes your "good buddy." And finally, the repairs fail and you threaten to sue the "quack" who tried to fix your swing. It is important to remember that correcting a swing flaw takes time, practice, repetition, and patience.

In the later chapters you will often visit this repair facility, but for putting, only the most severe problems will be addressed. The reason is that the vast majority of putting errors are caused by negative thoughts—"I'm going to miss this putt," "I can't putt," or "I stink"—and not by mechanical flaws. The Mechanic reluctantly discusses putting mishaps because thinking about putting usually causes more putting problems. The solution for most putting problems is the frequent practice of short putts (two to three feet) that improve your putting stroke and build your confidence. Specific putting problems will be addressed in the Repair Shop in the next chapter.

The Golf Guy: Talking Like a Golfer

Golfers have created a special language for putting. The following is a conversation I had with a fellow golfer who asked, "Mark, how did you play?". Translations of "putterese" are given in the parentheses.

Okay, but I couldn't make any putts (I am a lousy putter). The first two putts I pulled (hit left). After a quick adjustment I pushed (hit right) the next two. On three holes the ball lipped out (hit the edge of the cup and rolled out). I had two putts that I babied (hit short of the hole) and a couple that needed to hit a house (hit too hard and ended up past the cup). A couple of putts hit spike marks (imprints left by golf shoes) and I once hit someone's ball mark (a coin or plastic chip used to mark the position of a golf ball). If I could have made some of those putts (whining), I would have shot even par (loss of contact with reality).

Ms. Etiquette: The Golf Bible

Every four years the major golf organizations revise and publish *The Rules of Golf*. This invaluable, inexpensive book describes the rules and etiquette guidelines of the game. The primary purpose of *The Rules of Golf* is to promote uniformity of play. Golfers are often confronted by situations in which they must refer to the rules book. Given the complexity and specificity of the rules, most golfers carry *The Rules of Golf* in their golf bag. If your golfing adventures continue beyond this book, you should purchase a copy.

The etiquette guidelines of golf promote safety, respect for other players, and course care. Throughout the book, Ms. Etiquette will teach you how to behave like a proper golfer. Another way to learn the proper course etiquette is to observe the behavior of skilled golfers, such as the golf professionals on television. Pay particular attention to the caddies: they are the ones who do most of the work.

Reward

For achieving the level of a closet putter, your reward will be a practice putting cup. An inexpensive practice putting hole can be purchased at any golf supplies store. The putting cup will provide you with practice putting to a regulation sized target.

15

Closing Thoughts

Can you complete the Training Center exercises in one session? It's not likely. Should you try to complete the skills test in one session? No! Take one skill, work on it, develop it, and then praise yourself for your efforts. How fast you learn the skills is not as important as how well you learn them. Remember, successful practice leads to successful golfing.

Chapter Three
Putting: Outdoors

Putting is like wisdom, partly a natural gift and partly the accumulation of experience.

–Arnold Palmer

It is time for you to go public and let the world know that you are a golfer. In this chapter you will take your blossoming putting stroke out to the golf course. Don't worry! You are just going to practice and not play a round of golf.

Why so much practice with the putter? The primary reason is the impact putting has on your overall score. Although the expected number of putts per hole is two, most beginners average between three and four putts a hole. That translates into fifty-four to seventy-two strokes per round of golf. If practice can reduce the number of putts by ten to thirty percent, your score average would drop by five to twenty-one strokes. Putting produces the greatest improvement in scoring performance in the shortest period of time.

There are other reasons to emphasize putting. First, putting is the great equalizer—one good putt can make up for several bad shots. Moreover, matches are won or lost on the putting green, and putting is a nondiscriminating skill: that is, physical stature or strength is not a factor in putting.

The Mechanic

Continued practice of putting will generate additional questions concerning the specifics of putting.

• My back hurts when I putt. What can I do?

Back pain and back injuries are common among golfers. To reduce the back pressure that occurs while putting, keep your knees flexed as you putt. Also, daily stretching is a good idea if you plan to play golf on a regular basis. The book, *Stretching*, by Bob Anderson, describes a variety of stretches and exercises for increasing flexibility and is an excellent resource.

• Where should I look when I putt?

As you prepare to putt, visualize an imaginary line from the target to the golf ball. Pick a spot on the line that is three inches ahead of the ball. When you putt look at that spot, and do not look at the hole until the ball passes over the spot.

• Some days I putt great and other days I can't "buy a putt." Why am I so inconsistent?

All golfers have good and bad putting days. A good putter will accept a bad day of putting while the poor putter will make all kinds of mechanical adjustments. If you are having one of those days, rebuild your confidence by working on the basics. For example, practice putts of six inches until you can make several in a row and then stop practicing. Remember to always conclude your practice session with a series of successful putts.

• *When I putt, I hear a miniature golfer inside my head giving me instructions such as, "Keep your wrists firm" and "Don't take your eye off the ball." Am I going nuts?*

Yes, you are! You have all the symptoms of a disorder known as golfing.

Psychologists label our internal voices as "self-talk." When we engage in a physical activity such as golf, our minds continually process how to perform strategies. Even as a beginner golfer you can appreciate why golf is called a mental game.

Since self-talk can interfere with performance, you must learn to control the little golfer inside your head. But can you stop self-talk? Probably not. If you tell yourself to stop thinking it will result in thinking about not thinking. Again, too much thinking.

The most effective approach for reducing the negative effects of self-talk is to take advantage of the mind's ability to create internal visual images. Visualization allows you to concentrate on the outcome rather than the process and can enhance your performance in most athletic endeavors.

☛ *Stop: Try This*

Take your putting cup, putter, and three golf balls to your indoor practice area. Stand five feet from the cup and attempt three putts. Before you hit each putt, visualize the ball rolling into the cup. Keep the image in your mind as you hit the ball.

Visualizing the putt

19

By concentrating on the image, your attention is focused on the outcome of the putt rather than the process of putting. Now, try integrating visualization into your practice drills. For example, before each chip shot visualize the ball landing on the green and rolling into the cup. You will discover that visualization will make the little golfer inside your head disappear and your performance improve.

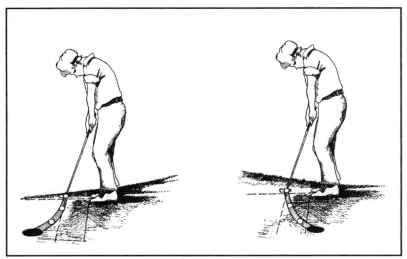

Reading the green

•How do I read the green?

The expression "reading the green" means determining the line and speed of a putt. The line of a putt refers to the direction of the putt (the ball will move to the right or left). The speed of the putt refers to how hard you must hit a putt.

Although experience is the best teacher for reading the green, there are some general guidelines to follow. First, consider the slope of the putt. Obviously, downhill putts are faster than uphill putts. Therefore, the easiest putts to make are uphill putts because they allow greater latitude in the speed of the putt. The slope can also influence the direction of the putt. Sidehill putts break with the direction of the slope.

A host of other variables can influence the line and speed of a putt. These factors include the type of grass, the grain of the grass, weather conditions, and the time of day. The only way to learn how these variables influence a putt is by putting. The number and magnitude of influencing variables may cause you to cringe, but with practice and experience you will quickly learn how to read a green.

• What do I do if I can't read a putt?

There will be occasions when you look at a putt and conclude that you don't know what the heck the putt is going to do. That happens to all golfers at some point. The strategy for that type of putt is to make a Faith putt. Aim at the center of the hole, hit the putt, and pray to the golf gods.

Practice Tips: Putting Strategy

The goal of putting is to get the ball in the hole with the fewest number of putts. To do that you need a game plan or putting strategy. The *KISSing Golf* putting strategy separates putts into three categories: No Problem putts, Maybe putts, and Dreamer putts. Each type of putt requires a different approach and goal.

• No Problem putts

A No Problem putt is a short putt of two feet or less. (A simple way to measure this putt is to use your putter. The distance between the putter grip and clubhead is approximately two feet.) The goal is to make this putt. With practice, putts of this length will be no problem.

21

• *Maybe putts*

Putts that range from two to seven feet are Maybe putts. The objective is to get these putts into the No Problem range and then make the short putt. Occasionally, you may be able to make these putts, but your overall objective is to take two strokes for a putt of this distance.

• *Dreamer putts*

If you think you can make a putt longer than seven feet, then you must be a dreamer. Your initial objective with any long putt is to get the ball inside the Maybe zone and then inside the No Problem range. Your goal is to take three strokes for any putt longer than seven feet.

The *KISSing Golf* putting strategy is to putt the ball from one putting range to the next closest zone. If you achieve this goal, you will never have more than three putts on any green. As your putting improves you can expand the range for No Problem and Maybe putts.

Training Center

The drills in this Training Center will refine your putting stroke and give you practice with the *KISSing Golf* putting strategy. As in the previous chapter, you will begin with short putts and move to progressively longer putts.

Training Center

Equipment Needed
- *Putter*
- *Three golf balls*

Task	Distance	Competence
☐ Putt ball into the hole while looking at the ball	2 feet	3 for 3
☐ Putt ball into the No Problem zone while looking at the hole	7 feet	2 for 3
☐ Putt ball into the No Problem zone while looking at the ball	7 feet	2 for 3
☐ Hit ball into the Maybe zone while looking at the hole	20 feet	2 for 3
☐ Hit ball into the Maybe zone while looking at the ball	20 feet	2 for 3

Repair Shop

As noted in the last chapter, most putting problems are caused by negative thoughts or overthinking. If the practice of short putts (No Problem putts) does not correct your putting difficulties, then identify your problem and use the corresponding treatment.

Symptom: Inconsistent direction control.
Treatment: The inability to control the direction of putts is usually due to misalignment. First, you need to check

the alignment of the putter to the target. The putter clubface should be aimed directly at the target. Second, you can check eye alignment with the "Golf Ball on My Nose" test. Assume your putting stance and prepare to putt a ball. Before you putt hold a golf ball against the bridge of your nose and drop the ball to the ground. If the ball hits the putting ball, then your eyes are properly aligned. If not, you will need

Golf ball on my nose

to change your posture until your eyes are directly aligned over the ball.

Symptom: Inconsistent distance control.
Treatment: Putting inconsistency is usually caused by an inconsistent putting stroke. One frequent cause of an inconsistent stroke is excessive wrist movement. There are several remedies: 1) increase the firmness of your grip, 2) concentrate on not allowing your

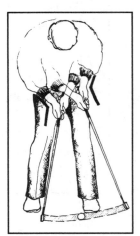

Accelerate through the ball

wrists to break down during the putt, 3) use more shoulder movement when you putt, and 4) accelerate through the ball.

The Golf Guy: Frustration

If you look up the word "frustration" in the dictionary, you will likely see a picture of a golfer next to the definition. The bottom line is that golf, particularly putting, is frustrating. The problem is that golfers often set their expectations higher than their ability level.

The *KISSing Golf* instructional program is designed for success. By achieving attainable goals, you will feel good about yourself and continue with the program. As you improve, you can modify your expectations. A friendly warning: don't modify your golfing expectations too quickly.

If you don't care for this psychological approach, you may prefer a method advocated by my golfing buddies to alleviate your frustration—the Jack Daniels treatment. Whenever you hit a bad shot, take a sip of Jack Daniels whiskey. After a few bad shots you will feel no frustration; in fact, you will not feel anything else!

Ms. Etiquette: Using a Practice Green

Unless you are filthy rich and fortunate enough to have a putting green in your backyard, you will have to go to a golf course to practice putting. Most golf courses, public and private, have a putting green that is used for practice purposes. Ask your friends or use the "Yellow Pages" to collect information about local courses and their practice facilities. Select a conveniently located public course that has a large, relatively flat practice green.

25

When you arrive at the course, you may have several questions concerning the use of the practice facilities.

• *Where is the practice green located?*

The practice green is usually located near the clubhouse and is easily identified by the multiple holes (with short flagsticks) placed throughout the green.

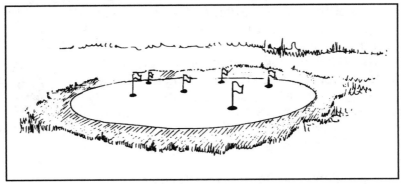

Practice green

• *Do I have to pay? Should I register or check in?*

No. Most public courses allow anyone to use the practice green. To be on the safe side you should ask at the clubhouse if there are any restrictions.

• *At which hole should I practice?*

Select a hole that is in a relatively flat area and is not being used by another player. Also, be careful not to step into the path of other players. After you complete the Training Center drills you can then practice at any hole.

• What do I wear to the golf course?

Although highly flammable polyester is the fabric of choice for most golfers, you can wear any comfortable, loose-fitting clothing. Some golf courses, however, have a dress code (such as, shirts with collars) and require golf shoes. The same etiquette used at restaurants should guide your clothing behavior: no shirt, no shoes, no golf.

Reward

Your reward for your persistence is a sleeve (or box) of three golf balls. Using the same brand of golf balls for putting will help improve your consistency. Select any brand that appeals to you and use these balls whenever you putt.

Closing Thoughts

This is the last chapter in which putting is discussed. It should not be, however, the last time that you practice putting. As stated before, putting is the most important golfing skill. Whenever you have extra time, practice putting with your new golf balls and putting cup.

Chapter Four
Chipping

> *If you watch a game, it's fun. If you play
> it, it's recreation. If you work at it, it's
> golf.*
>
> *—Bob Hope*

During a typical round of golf you will hit many shots that land near or short of the putting green. The recovery shot from off the green will travel a few yards in the air, land on the green, and roll up to the hole. That type of shot is called a chip shot.

The chip shot is an important skill to learn for several reasons. First, chipping will allow you to recover from less than perfect approach shots to the green, and these recovery shots can shave strokes off your overall score. Moreover, chipping will help you learn the full golf swing.

The Mechanic

Although the chip shot can be executed with most of the irons, you will use a pitching wedge or nine-iron. Let's have the Mechanic address the basics of chipping.

• *How do I hold the club?*

Place your left hand on the middle of the rubber grip. Moving the hands to the middle of the grip like this is known as "choking down." Grasp the club with a baseball, interlocking, or overlapping grip as illustrated in Chapter Two. The club should be held in the palm of the left hand and the last three fingers of the right hand. The thumbs will rest on the opposite sides of the rubber grip.

Grip pressure is increased for the chip shot, with approximately three-four on the grip pressure scale described in the second chapter. This firmer grip will prevent excessive wrist action and lead to better consistency and results. It is very important that you maintain the same degree of grip pressure during the entire shot.

• *How do I aim?*

The grip, club, and body must be properly aligned to execute a successful shot. First, the grip is aligned by pointing the "v" formed by the left thumb and index finger to a spot

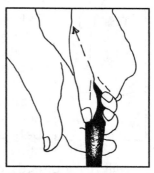

Left hand alignment

between the head and right shoulder. The right hand is placed on the club using an interlocking, overlapping, or baseball grip. The "v" formed by the right thumb and index finger should also point to a spot between your head and right shoulder. Ideally, the palms face each other and the "v's" of both hands point to the same location.

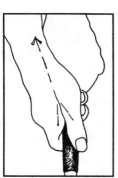

Right hand alignment

The second alignment consideration is the position of the club relative to the target. The clubface is placed directly behind the ball and aimed at the target. Hand alignment should be checked after the club is pointed at the target.

The final alignment step is the position of the body relative to the target. Body alignment has a significant impact on the direction of a shot, particularly for the mini-swing and full swing, and will be discussed in detail in the next two chapters.

• *How do I stand?*

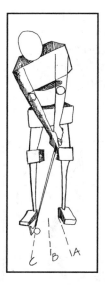

Stand with your feet approximately twelve to eighteen inches apart. Pull the left foot back a few inches to create an open stance. (A closed stance occurs when the left foot is slightly ahead of the right foot.) The open stance will promote freer arm and shoulder movement.

The ball is placed across from the insole of the right foot (ball position C). The hands are positioned several inches in front of the ball (hand position A) to facilitate a descending stroke.

To establish proper posture and alleviate lower back pressure slightly flex your knees, bend from the hips, stick out your behind, and keep your back relatively straight. If your posture is correct, your arms will hang directly down from your shoulders, and your hands will be a few inches in front of your thighs.

• *How do I swing?*

The chip shot is a pendulum arm swing with little wrist action or body movement. The left hand guides the shot and must always stay ahead of the club during the stroke. If the club leads the shot, your left wrist will collapse and you will not be able to chip the ball off the ground.

The length of your swing is directly related to how far you want to hit the ball. For short chip shots, take a very short backswing. When you want to hit the ball further take a slightly longer backswing. If you are swinging the club above your waist for a chip shot, your swing is too long.

To get the ball off the ground you must do the opposite of what your instincts tell you to do; that is, do not try to lift the ball up. To get the ball airborne you must hit down and through the ball. If you hit the ball in a descending and sweeping motion, the ball will pop off the ground. You also must restrict excessive body movement and the tendency to look up quickly at the result.

Let's review the pre-shot routine for a chip shot. First, you must identify a target. The target will typically be a spot on the green that is approximately one-third of the distance to the hole.

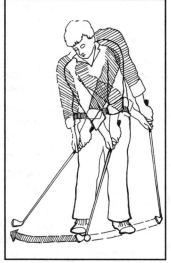

Chipping stroke

The goal is to land the ball on the spot and have the ball roll up to the hole. Think of a chip shot has having two parts—a short shot combined with a putt.

After the target has been identified, the shot becomes a GASS. Grip the club in the middle of the rubber grip with an interlocking, overlapping, or baseball grip. Align the hands to a point between the head and right shoulder, aim the club at the target, and position the body to the left of the target. Stand in a relaxed posture with the arms hanging naturally down. Swing the club using a pendulum-like stroke without excessive wrist or body movement.

31

•*What are the irons?*

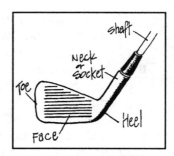

The irons have a thin, metal clubhead with a steel or graphite shaft. The irons can be classified as short irons, middle irons, or long irons. The short irons consist of the eight-iron, nine-iron, pitching wedge (ten-iron), sand wedge (eleven-iron), and lob wedge (twelve-iron). The middle irons consist of the five-iron, six-iron, and seven-iron. The long irons consist of the one-iron, two-iron, three-iron, and four-iron.

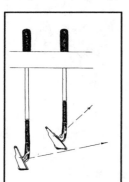

The numbering system used to identify golf clubs reflect the clubhead loft (which influences the trajectory or height of a shot) and the length of the shaft. For example, a low number, such as one or two, is used for a club that produces a long shot with low trajectory. To illustrate, let's compare the nine-iron to the five-iron. The nine-iron is a shorter club with more loft and will produce a high, short shot, while the five-iron will yield a lower, longer shot. Unfortunately, the numbering system does not allow for direct comparisons between the woods and irons. That is, a three-wood is not the same as a three-iron.

Training Center

As with the putting drills, you first practice indoors with short shots and gradually progress to longer ones. When you become comfortable with chipping, move outdoors to the practice green.

Chipping ✔ *List*

Grip

❑ "Choke-down" on the club (hands on the middle of the grip).

❑ Hold the club with an interlocking, overlapping, or baseball grip.

❑ Maintain constant grip pressure.

Alignment

❑ Aim the clubface toward the target.

❑ Point the v's of both hands to a spot between the head and right shoulder.

❑ Align the body to the left of the target.

Stance

❑ Stand with the feet close together (12-16 inches).

❑ Pull the left foot back to create an open stance.

❑ Position the ball toward the right foot (ball position C).

❑ Place the hands near the left thigh (hand position A).

❑ Bend the knees.

Swing

❑ Accelerate through the shot.

❑ Clip the ball off the ground.

❑ Make the forward swing longer than the backswing.

Training Center

Equipment Needed
- *Pitching wedge or nine-iron*
- *Putter*
- *Three tennis balls*
- *Three golf balls*

Task	Distance	Competence
❏ Chip tennis ball over golf ball	3 feet	3 for 3
❏ Chip golf ball over tennis ball	3 feet	3 for 3
❏ Chip golf ball on green	2 yards	2 for 3
❏ Chip golf ball on green	4 yards	2 for 3
❏ Chip golf ball into the Dreamer zone	2 yards	2 for 3
❏ Chip golf ball into Maybe zone	3 yards	1 for 3

Repair Shop

Poor mechanics will prevent you from developing a feel for chipping and reduce your consistency. The following are the two most common chipping errors and their corresponding remedies.

Symptom: Cannot chip the ball off the ground.
Treatment: To get the ball airborne the hands must be ahead of the club at impact. Before the shot the hands are located across from the inside of the left leg (hand position A) while the ball is across from the inside of the right foot (position C). During the swing the hands must remain ahead of the club. If the wrists break down at impact (the flippy wrist syndrome), the club will be ahead of the hands. The flippy wrist can be prevented by increasing the firmness of your grip, concentrating on not allowing your wrists to break down during the shot, and using more arm and shoulder movement when you chip.

Symptom: Inconsistent distance control.
Treatment: Beginners often take too much of a backswing and compensate by slowing-up, or decelerating, the club as it reaches the ball. A simple cure is to make sure the forward swing is as long, or longer, than the backswing.

Practice Tips: Developing a Swing Routine

A pre-shot swing routine can improve your consistency and swing tempo, reduce tension, and discourage the tendency to become too mechanical. Although there is no one correct swing routine, the following are the typical components of a pre-shot routine.

• *Practice swing*

Before you hit a shot, any shot, take a practice swing. The purpose of the practice swing is to tell your muscles what you expect them to do. It is also a good idea to look at the target while taking the practice swing. Focusing on the target during your practice swing will remind you that distance and direction are the keys to any successful shot.

• Movement

Beginners will often stand over a ball for an indefinite period of time before swinging. It is extremely difficult to hit a golf ball from a static position. To promote a fluid and flowing swing, you must keep moving up to the point of beginning the swing. Think of the pre-shot movement as "ants in your pants." Move your feet, waggle the club, and slide into the swing.

• Consistency

The final element of a good swing routine is consistency. Although there is no one correct pre-shot routine, each movement of your routine must occur in the same sequence and at the same rate. Whatever your individual routine is, it needs to be repeatable.

The Golf Guy: How Golf Balls Really Feel

Golfers often form unusual, sometimes pathological relationships with their golf balls. To help understand this relationship the Golf Guy conducted interviews with golf balls of different creeds and backgrounds. The following observations are the thoughts and feelings of golf balls in their own words.

Don't blame us for your mistakes. If you are a bad golfer, it's not our fault. And there is no conspiracy against you—it's not like we get together and plan to sabotage your golf game. By the way, switching golf balls is not going to make you a better golfer.

Please don't discriminate. There is nothing more demeaning than to be picked as the mercy ball for an ill-fated attempt over a water hazard. Even though we may not be of equal monetary value, we believe all golf balls are created equal. If you are going to drown one of us, please randomly select the victim. Also, we would really appreciate a moment to say goodbye to our friends.

We like our privacy. If you are having difficulty locating a ball, did you ever consider that maybe we didn't want to come back? There are times we like to be alone and enjoy the great outdoors. So if you find one of us resting, say under a leaf, respect our right to private time and leave us alone.

Practice good ball hygiene. When you are dirty, you take the time to clean yourself. We would appreciate similar treatment.

Ms. Etiquette: Proper Behavior for the Putting Green

How well behaved are you? The following quiz will help you learn the rules and etiquette associated with the putting green. Try to answer the items before peeking at the answers.

1) Who putts first on the putting green?
2) What is a ball marker? What does a ball marker allow you to do?
3) What is a ball mark? What is a ball impression repairer?
4) Do you leave the flagstick in or take it out when you putt?
5) What are the pet peeves of golfers preparing to putt?

Answers

1) The rules of golf state that the person farthest from the hole hits first. For example, assume Player A is in a greenside bunker 15 feet away and Player B is on the green 25 feet away. Most golfers believe that since Player A is off the green, she should hit first. That is incorrect: Player B is farthest away, so she must go first. Remember that distance determines the order of play, not the location of the ball. (There are, however, times when the rule may be ignored to speed up the rate of play.)

2) A ball marker is a small, flat object, such as a coin, that is used to mark the location of the ball on the green. Marking the ball allows you to pick up the ball and clean it. The ball marker also allows you to remove your ball so it does not interfere with the shot of another player.

   The procedure for marking is simple. Place the marker immediately behind the ball and lift the ball. If the marker interferes with the path of another player's putt, use your putter clubhead to mark the ball to the left or right of the original spot. To replace the ball, place it on the original spot and remove the marker.

3) A ball mark, or ball impression, often occurs when a ball hits the green. To repair the damage, push a tee or divot repair tool (an inexpensive device available at golf stores) under the impression and lift the ground until it is even with the green. Level off the ball mark by tamping down with your putter.

4) The rules of golf state that the ball should not strike the flagstick when playing from the green. You have two options. The first is to remove the flagstick and place it in a safe location where the flagstick will not interfere with anyone's putt. The second is to ask your playing partner to hold or "attend" the flagstick until you hit the putt, then remove it as the ball approaches the hole. There is

no penalty for a ball hitting the flagstick when the shot is played from off the green.

5) Proper etiquette around the green includes not talking or moving while others are putting, staying around the green until the final player completes putting, and replacing the flagstick when play is completed.

Reward

Wouldn't it be nice to practice golf in the backyard without worrying about breaking a window or injuring a loved one? The reward for this chapter is a set of practice golf balls constructed of plastic or foam rubber. The foam rubber balls with a solid center last longer and provide a better representation of the actual flight of a golf shot.

Closing Thoughts

Most golfers keep a putter and wedge around for practice because it is easy to squeeze in a few minutes of putting and chipping. A few minutes of practice each day will greatly improve your golfing ability and lower your scoring average.

Chapter Five
Pitching

> *The pleasure derived from hitting a ball*
> *dead center on the club is comparable*
> *only to one or two other pleasures that*
> *come to mind at the moment.*
>
> *—Unknown*

In the previous chapters you learned the skills needed for shots on and around the putting green. To put those skills to use you must first get the ball to the green. In this chapter you will learn the skills needed for the pitch

A chip shot

A pitch shot

40

shot. The primary difference between pitching and chipping is the trajectory and length of the shot. A chip shot
has a low trajectory and is hit to the green from a distance of 10 yards or less. The pitch shot has a higher
trajectory and is hit from 10 yards and farther. The pitch
shot has more air time and less ground time than a chip
shot.

The Mechanic

Let's discuss the fundamentals of pitching.

• *How do I hold the club?*

Grasp the club near the top of the rubber grip with
an interlocking, overlapping, or baseball grip. A light grip,
with a grip pressure scale rating of two to three, that
allows the muscles of the hands and forearms to relax
will promote a more fluid swing. It is important not to
regrip the club during the swing and alter the grip pressure.

• *How do I aim?*

First, the grip is aligned by
pointing the "v's" of both hands to
a spot between your head and right
shoulder. The club is primarily held
in the palm of the left hand and the
last three fingers of the right hand.
The palms of the hands should face
each other.

Next, the clubface is placed directly behind the ball and aimed at
the target. The grip should be rechecked to assure that the hands
are still properly aligned. Finally, the
body is aligned to the left of the

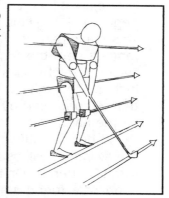

Proper alignment

41

target and parallel to the target line (the imaginary line from the ball to the target). Visualize a series of poles going through your shoulders, hips, and feet. Each of the poles should be parallel to the target line. If any part of the body is not properly aligned to the target, the attempted shot will likely go off line. An important practice drill for establishing body alignment is described in the Practice Tips section.

• How do I stand?

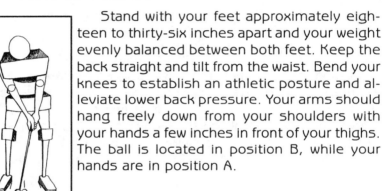

Stand with your feet approximately eighteen to thirty-six inches apart and your weight evenly balanced between both feet. Keep the back straight and tilt from the waist. Bend your knees to establish an athletic posture and alleviate lower back pressure. Your arms should hang freely down from your shoulders with your hands a few inches in front of your thighs. The ball is located in position B, while your hands are in position A.

• How do I swing?

The mini-swing is an abbreviated swing that will be used for pitch shots and practice drills. The swing begins with the club moving straight away from the ball. This initial path, or takeaway, of the club is very important—it sets the tone for the entire swing. The club is swung straight back and low to the ground for several inches. The takeaway is a slow, sweeping movement that is controlled by the left arm and shoulder and not by the hands.

To help identify proper position at different points of the swing we will use the visualization of shaking hands with two friends. On the backswing, imagine shaking the hand of a friend standing on your right with your left hand. On the forward swing, you will shake the hand of the person to the left with your right hand. Let's discuss these checkpoints in the context of the entire swing.

When the club is parallel to the ground during the backswing, the tip or toe of the club should point straight up. At this checkpoint, the backside of the left hand should be facing away from the body and be parallel to the target line. You should be able to shake someone's hand standing on the right with your left hand.

Depending on the distance of the shot, the backswing continues to a point where the hands reach between chest and shoulder height. A frequent mistake is to con-sciously bend, or cock, the wrists. With the proper grip pressure of two to three, the wrists will reflexively bend and be in position for the forward swing.

The forward swing begins as a natural response to the swinging back of the club. The hands and arms lead the downswing with the body responding to the motion. At ball impact, the club returns to its original, square position.

After the ball is struck, the hands and arms move to the left side. When the club reaches the point of being parallel to the ground during the forward swing, the toe of the club should point straight up and the backside of

Mini-swing

the right hand should face away from the body and be parallel to the target line. At this checkpoint you should be able to shake someone's hand standing on the left with your right hand. To assure that you are hitting or accelerating through the shot, the hands should continue to at least shoulder height on the forward swing.

Most golfers equate power with swing speed. Although clubhead speed is related to the distance of a shot, clubhead speed is generated by the leverage of proper body mechanics and not a fast tempo. If you lose your balance when you swing, you are swinging too fast.

The basic goal of any golf shot is to swing the club back and return the clubface to its original position at ball impact. The short strokes of putting and chipping simplify that challenge. The arm swing and body movement needed for the mini-swing and full swing complicate the process. The increased complexity of the mini-swing means that it will take you longer to acquire this skill than the time needed to learn putting and chipping.

Practice Tips: Building a Practice Area

A simple and easy way to improve direction control is to create a practice area that facilitates proper body

and club alignment. You will need two clubs, in addition to the club you are hitting with, to build a practice zone. The first club is placed on the ground and aimed at the target. The second club is placed two feet inside of, and parallel to, the target club (like a set of railroad tracks).

Balls are hit between the two clubs. The outside, or target club, is used to align the clubface to the target. The club nearest to you helps you align your shoulders, hips, legs, and feet parallel to the target. By building a

Pitching ✔ *List*

Grip

❑ Place the hands one inch below the top of the club.
❑ Rest the thumbs on the opposite sides of the grip.
❑ Grasp the club with an interlocking, overlapping, or baseball grip.
❑ Maintain constant grip pressure (levels two to three) during the swing.

Alignment

❑ Point the v's of both hands between the head and right shoulder.
❑ Aim the clubface toward the target.
❑ Align the shoulders, hips, and feet parallel to the target.

Stance

❑ Stand with the feet approximately twelve to sixteen inches apart.
❑ Position the ball in the middle of the stance (ball position B).
❑ Place the hands ahead of the ball near the left thigh (hand position A).
❑ Bend the knees.
❑ Distribute weight evenly between the left and right side.

Swing

❑ Use an arm-oriented swing with natural body movement.
❑ Swing the club to chest level on the backswing.
❑ Swing the club to head level on the forward swing.

practice zone, you will quickly learn how to properly align the club and your body to the target.

Training Center

The remaining training sessions will occur outdoors. Unless you have an usually large yard or access to a uncrowded field or park, you will need to go to a driving range to practice the skills in the remainder of the book.

When selecting a driving range, there are several factors to consider. First, try to avoid ranges that use artificial turf. Golf is always played on natural turf, so you should always practice on grass. Second, consider the cost of a bag or bucket of balls. Prices can vary by several dollars so it is worth bargain hunting. Third, check the types of practice balls that are used; some driving ranges use "experienced" (used) balls that are so damaged that the balls act strangely when you hit them.

The initial training exercise helps you develop your ability to hit the ball by practicing with tennis balls. After you feel comfortable with the mini-swing, the practice drills will require you to pitch golf balls for progressively longer distances.

Repair Shop

As you progress from the chip shot to the pitch shot there is an increased likelihood of mistakes. Fortunately, making pre-shot corrections is the quickest and most efficient strategy for fixing swing mishaps. If you encounter problems pitching the ball, use the ✔ list to make sure you are properly set up. If that fails, use the following remedies for your pitching problems.

Symptom: Hitting the top of the ball.
Treatment: Topping the ball is caused by having the ball too far forward in the stance (ball position A instead of

Training Center

Equipment Needed
• *Pitching wedge (or nine-iron)*
• *Practice golf balls*
• *Three tennis balls*

Task	Distance	Competence
☐ Hit tennis ball with mini-swing	Any	3 for 3
☐ Hit golf ball with mini-swing	Any	3 for 3
☐ Hit golf ball airborne	Any	2 for 3
☐ Pitch the ball	10 yards	2 for 3
☐ Pitch the ball	20 yards	2 for 3
☐ Pitch the ball	30 yards	1 for 3

ball position B) or by lifting up the body or head during the swing. To treat topping, move the ball back to the middle of the stance and keep your head still during the swing. The expression "keep your eyes on the ball" is partially correct—you obviously want to watch the ball, but you also must make sure that your head doesn't significantly move during the swing. Beginners are often so anxious to see the results of their efforts that they look up before they hit the shot.

Symptom: Inconsistent distance control.
Treatment: If the length and intensity of your swing changes from shot to shot, you will have difficulty controlling the distance of each shot. A common mistake is to slow up, or decelerate, during the forward swing. Try to maintain the same swing speed for all shots and accelerate through each shot. However, this does not mean that you should swing fast. Allow the length of the swing, not the speed of the swing, to dictate the distance of the shot.

Symptom: Inconsistent direction control.
Treatment: Shots hit off line are usually due to poor alignment. The drill previously described in the Practice Tips outlines ways to check your alignment.

The Golf Guy: Do You Suffer From Golfitis?

Golfitis is an insidious disease that slowly overtakes its victims. Hopefully, the following list of symptoms will help you recognize whether you are falling victim to golfitis and prevent you being admitted to The Center for the Golf Inflicted. You suffer from golfitis if you:

- Replace your favorite romantic fantasy with a dream of a hole-in-one.
- Pray more at the golf course than at church.

- Say, "I can do that," after watching a golf professional hit a perfect shot.
- Talk to your golf balls and believe that they listen.
- Believe that a new putter would really help your putting.
- Feel your most intimate relation with God occurs on the golf course.
- Believe that luck plays no role in a good shot.
- Prefer last rites to be administered by your golf professional.
- Prefer good golf to good sex.
- Prefer bad golf to good sex.

Ms. Etiquette: Proper Behavior at the Driving Range

The following are guidelines for appropriate etiquette during your practice at a driving range:

Be respectful of others. Maintain an appropriate distance from other golfers so that you do not interfere with their swing. Although talking is permitted, try not to disturb other golfers.

Be respectful of the driving range. Practice from designated areas (usually marked with ropes or lines). Also, with the mini-swing and full swing you will automatically hit the turf so hard that you will remove a piece of sod or "take a divot." Although it is your responsibility on the course to pick up the divot and replace the turf in its original spot, replacing divots at a driving range is usually not convenient or possible. To help maintain the condition of the driving range, it is recommended that you try not to take divots with your practice swings.

Promote safety. Avoid the tendency to collect shots that only travel a few yards—many golfers have been hit while scavenging for additional practice balls.

Reward

The reward for this chapter is a golf glove. Most right-handed golfers wear a glove on their left hand to improve their grip of the club and protect their hand from blisters and calluses. The most important factor in selecting a glove is its fit: the glove should fit snugly yet not restrict finger movement.

Closing Thoughts

Putts, chip shots, and pitch shots comprise the "short game." Because of the importance of the short game, you should imitate the practice habits of golf professionals, who devote two-thirds of their practice time to the short game, which is the fastest way to improve your score.

Chapter Six
The Full Swing

*For most amateurs, the best wood in
the bag is the pencil.*

—Chi Chi Rodriguez

The first shot on a golf hole is played from a small area designated as the "teeing area" or "tee box." The teeing area is the only part of the course in which you are allowed the advantage of teeing the ball. Since the green is usually unreachable from the teeing area, except on par three's, the goal of the first shot is to hit the ball long and straight into the fairway. The shot itself is

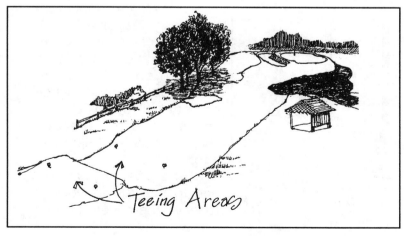

often referred to as the "drive" because the club most frequently used from the teeing area is the driver (#1 wood). In this chapter, you will learn how to use the full swing to hit a drive.

The Mechanic

It's an easy transition from the mini-swing to the full swing.

• Which club do I use?

Most golfers experience problems with the driver because of self-defeating thoughts and the specifications of the one-wood. The destructive thoughts that produce the driving woes fall into one of the following two categories.

First, most golfers become ego-involved with their driver. The length of their shots seems to be directly tied to their sense of golfhood. To be a real golfer you must hit the ball as far as possible. By placing a premium on length rather than control, these golfers adversely alter their swings by trying to "kill" the ball.

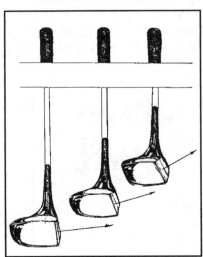

Second, the shot from the teeing area can be intimidating. All of the members of your group and other players are gathered around to watch you hit. Performance anxiety will often lead to choking and the dreaded "swing, miss, and spin like a top" shot.

The *KISSing Golf* solution to the driving woes is to leave the driver at home

Driver, 3-wood, 5-wood

and replace it with the five-wood. Some beginners resist using the five-wood because of their obsession with distance. It is true that you may not be able to hit the ball as far with the five-wood, but say to yourself, "So what if my friend can hit the ball farther. Golf success is measured by a lower score, not by the distance of one shot."

• *How do I hold the club?*

Grasp the club near the top of the rubber grip with a baseball, interlocking, or overlapping grip. Your grip should be firm enough (grip pressure scale of two to three) to hold onto the club but not a death grip—you are not trying to strangle the club. It is important to maintain the same grip pressure intensity throughout the entire swing.

• *How do I aim?*

The alignment procedure remains the same for the full swing. First, the "v's" of both hands are pointed to a spot between the head and right shoulder. Next, the club is placed directly behind the ball, and the clubface aimed at the target. Then, the grip should be rechecked to assure that the hands are still properly aligned. Finally, the shoulders, hips, and feet are aligned parallel to the target line.

• *How do I stand?*

The stance is wider for the full swing—your feet should be approximately shoulder-width apart. The wider stance promotes a longer swing by allowing the hips and legs to be integrated into the swing. The wider stance also provides greater stability for the full swing.

As the clubs become longer, the ball is moved forward in the stance. For the five-wood, the ball is located across from the insole of the left foot (ball position A).

53

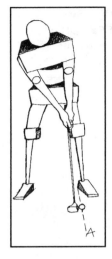

The hands are even with, or slightly ahead, of the ball (hand position A). The position of your hands relative to your left thigh should remain constant for all the clubs. Although the longer club will alter your posture by forcing you to stand more upright, the basics of the stance remain the same. The knees are slightly flexed, the waist bent, and the arms hanging naturally down. The weight is evenly distributed between the left and right feet. With the ball and hands in position A, the right shoulder will be lower than the left shoulder.

• *How do I swing?*

The full swing is an extension of the mini-swing and will be used for every long shot. The mini-swing and the full swing both begin with a takeaway that has the club moving in a straight path away from the ball. The takeaway is a slow, sweeping movement that is dominated by the left arm and shoulder. When the hands reach the point of being parallel to the ground, the backside of the left hand should be parallel to the target line

Full swing with a wood

(you should be able to shake someone's hand standing to the right with your left hand).

One of the key differences between the full swing and the mini-swing is the length of the backswing. For the mini-swing, the backswing ends when the hands reach chest level. For the full swing, the backswing continues until the hands are at approximately head level. As you swing back, the left shoulder turns under the chin.

Transfer of weight in full swing

An important element of the full swing is the transfer of weight that occurs during the swing. The swing begins with the weight evenly distributed between the right and left feet. The backswing is accompanied by a gradual shift of weight to the right side. At the top of the backswing, the majority of your weight will be on the right side. The flexed right knee serves as an anchor to support the hip and shoulder turn. The pressure of the weight transfer is felt on the inside of the right foot and leg. At the

top of the backswing you will feel like you are wound up like a top.

The forward swing begins as a reflexive response to being wound up like a top. Let the arms and hands lead the uncurling of the body. During the forward swing, a reverse transfer of weight from the right to left side occurs. At the conclusion of the swing the majority of your weight should be on the left foot.

Most golfers do not hit their woods consistently because they mistakenly believe that the long club and larger clubhead requires a faster swing. The swing speed, or tempo, remains the same for all clubs. It is true that the longer club will produce a longer swing arc; however, the pace of the swing remains the same. In other words, you should swing the five-wood at the same tempo you used for the wedge.

The rotation and lateral move that is required by the full swing is influenced by body shape, flexibility, and coordination. The balance and timing that is required by the weight transfer during the swing is a complex motor skill that takes time and practice to acquire. Recognizing the complexity of the full swing will hopefully foster patience in developing this skill.

• *How high do I tee up the ball?*

As a fairway wood, the five-wood can be hit off the turf or teed up. When a tee is used, the ball is teed so that the top half of the ball is above the clubhead.

Teeing the ball

Full Swing ✔ List

Grip

- ❑ Place the left hand one inch below the top of the club.
- ❑ Place the thumbs on the opposite sides of the grip.
- ❑ Use a baseball, interlocking, or overlapping grip.
- ❑ Maintain constant grip pressure (levels two or three) throughout the swing.

Alignment

- ❑ Point the v's of both hands to between the head and right shoulder.
- ❑ Aim the clubface toward the target.
- ❑ Align the shoulders, hips, and feet parallel to the target.

Stance

- ❑ Stand with the feet approximately shoulder-width apart.
- ❑ Position the ball off the inside of the left foot (ball position A).
- ❑ Place the hands slightly ahead of the ball (hand position A).
- ❑ Flex the knees and place weight on balls of feet.
- ❑ Bend at the hips.
- ❑ Distribute weight evenly between the left and right side.

Swing

- ❑ Use a chin-to-shoulder swing (hands swung to shoulder level).
- ❑ Use an arm-oriented swing with natural body movement.
- ❑ Transfer weight during the swing.

Practice Tips: Avoiding Machine Gun Practice

Many golfers never develop a good swing because of their practice habits. Rather than using their practice time productively, they waste their efforts with "machine gun" practice sessions (rapidly hitting one shot after another). Hitting balls just for the sake of hitting balls is of little value.

The ideal practice session has a purpose. If you treat each practice session as a learning lesson, you will be golfing in no time at all. An outline of the ideal practice session is described on the next page.

The last point in the Practice Session is particularly important: always finish the practice session with a successful shot. Once you have found a good swing, stop practicing. Even though you may have paid for fifty balls, you do not have to hit all the balls. Don't allow the cheapskate inside you to forget that the quality of practice is more important than the quantity of practice.

Training Center

The training drills will build your swing confidence by first practicing with the mini-swing. After you develop consistent ball striking skills using the mini-swing, you will progress to the full swing. The drills will alternate using a tee and hitting the ball off the ground.

Repair Shop

Golfers have developed a special language to describe the infinite numbers of less than perfect shots. The following list identifies some of the terms that golfers use to communicate, correct, and whine about their ugly-looking shots.

Ideal Practice Session

I. Warm-up Period (five minutes)
• Complete stretching exercises.
• Swing slowly two to three clubs.
• Hit ten mini-swing shots with a wedge or nine-iron.

II. Training Period (ten minutes)
• Build a practice zone by laying down clubs down for alignment.
• Identify a specific skill to develop.
• Concentrate on the swing mechanics and ignore the outcome.
• Take a practice swing before every shot.
• Avoid machine-gun tendencies by hitting one ball no more than every minute.

III. Find-a-Swing Period (fifteen minutes)
• Concentrate on distance control and ignore swing mechanics.
• Select a target for each shot.
• Look at the target as you take a practice swing.
• Try to feel your swing.
• Use the mini-swing to find your swing tempo. and build success.
• Take a break or change clubs when you become frustrated.
• End the practice session with a successful shot.

Training Center

Equipment Needed
•*Five-wood (or three-wood)*
•*Golf tees*

Task	Distance	Competence
☐ Hit golf ball with mini-swing using a tee	Any	3 for 3
☐ Hit golf ball with full swing using a tee	Any	3 for 3
☐ Hit golf ball airborne with mini-swing using a tee	Any	2 for 3
☐ Hit golf ball airborne with full swing using tee	Any	2 for 3
☐ Hit golf ball airborne without a tee	Any	2 for 3

Shot Characteristic

Names

Ball rolls along
the ground

Shank, topped, dribbler,
gopher killer, grounder,
worm burner

Ball hit high in the air

Skied, rain maker, pop-
up

Ball is missed

Strike out, windmill, whiff

Ball curves to the
right of the target

Slice, fade, cut, push

Ball curves to the
left of the target

Hook, draw, pull

If practice with the five-wood produces a consistent
pattern of poor shots, then you can try the remedies
listed below. Do not waste your time readjusting your
swing when the mishits are infrequent. Making numer-
ous swing changes can make a swing problem worse
rather than better. If you get frustrated, quit the five-
wood and hit a few pitch shots to regain your confidence.

Learning how to self-correct your swing is an important step to becoming a good golfer. The GASS (grip,
alignment, stance, and swing) diagnostic procedure
should be used to analyze swing problems. It is important to remember that most swing mistakes are due to
poor grip, alignment, and set-up. Always check your pre-
shot mechanics before making swing corrections.

Symptom: Shanking.
Grip: Relax the grip and maintain the same grip pressure
throughout the swing.
Alignment: Usually not a contributing factor.

5tance: Move away from the ball so the hands are three to four inches from the left thigh.
5wing: Concentrate on swinging the club down the line toward the target.

Symptom: Topping.
Grip: Relax your grip and maintain the same grip pressure throughout the swing.
Alignment: Usually not a contributing factor.
5tance: Move the ball closer to ball position B.
5wing: Hold the head steady and maintain the same right knee flex throughout the swing.

Symptom: Skying.
Grip: Relax your grip pressure.
Alignment: Usually not a contributing factor.
5tance: Move the ball back in the stance, or move closer to the ball to promote a more upright stance.
5wing: Concentrate on keeping your head at the same height through the swing.

The Golf Guy: It's Not Your Fault

Golfs balls are dumb creatures: They will only go where you direct them to go. That means that any putt or shot hit poorly was your fault. Does that mean you should take responsibility for your less than desired shots? Absolutely not! Your job is to find excuses for the bad shots. The following are some tried and tested explanations for those occasional mistakes:

• Obviously, that was a defective ball.
• I was trying to do that.

- Did you see that wasp flying around my head?
- You know, I was thinking about global warming when I hit that shot. It was not a great shot, but at least I came up with several possible solutions to the world's problems.
- My doctor said the change in my medication might affect my swing.
- My hair fell into my eyes. Do you think I need to cut my bangs?

Ms. Etiquette: How to Avoid Being Busted

The most often committed golf felony is slow play. The crime occurs so often that many courses employ "rangers" to monitor the rate of play. Slow players will receive a warning, and repeat offenders might be asked to leave the course. The required etiquette when playing slow is to allow faster golfers to play through, which means standing aside on a hole and informing the players behind you to hit and move ahead of your group.

Improving your rate of play can be practiced at the driving range. At the end of your practice time, play an imaginary hole. Picture yourself on a tee hitting into a fairway. Tee up the ball and use the five-wood for the first shot. For the second shot, visualize a green to shoot at. Decide on your club and complete your pre-shot routine and hit the shot. By playing imaginary holes you can practice computing the distance to a target, selecting a club, taking a practice swing, and hitting the shot. The goal is to speed up your rate of decision-making rather than your swing tempo.

Reward

The reward for this chapter is a golf magazine. There are a variety of golf magazines that offer instructional tips, equipment information, and a synopsis of golf news. Browse through the variety of golf magazines and pick the one that appeals to you.

Closing Thoughts

Often golfers say, "I don't have a swing today," or "I can't find my swing." These comments illustrate the elusive nature of the golf swing and that the real challenge of golf is learning how to play when you can't hit the ball worth a hoot. The *KiSSing Golf* philosophy maximizes your scoring ability by concentrating on the important part of golf—the short game. Remember, improving your putting and chipping can compensate for bad swing days.

Chapter Seven
Putting it Together

*Golf is life. If you can't take golf, you
can't take life.*

–Anonymous

So far you have practiced with three clubs: the putter, wedge, and five-wood. The rules of golf allow you to carry and use fourteen different clubs. In this chapter you will learn when and how to use the remaining clubs. As your skills blossom you will come to appreciate the value of using different clubs. For now, the *KISSing Golf* method encourages you to keep it simple—use as few clubs as possible. It is more important for you to experience success than to experience diversity.

The Mechanic

The Mechanic will explain how the different clubs will affect your swing.

• How do I hold the club?

Although the clubs are different, the grip remains the same. Grasp the club near the top of the rubber grip with a baseball, interlocking, or overlapping grip. A light, yet firm, grip should be maintained throughout the entire swing.

• *How do I aim?*

The alignment procedure remains the same for all the clubs. First, hold the club so that the "v's" of both hands point to a spot between the head and right shoulder. Then set the club directly behind the ball and

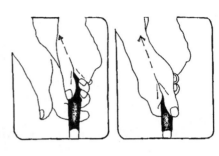

aim the clubface at the target. Finally, align the shoulders, hips, and feet to the left of the target and parallel to the target line.

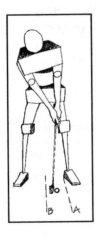

• *How do I stand?*

The feet should be approximately shoulder-width apart with the weight evenly distributed between the left and right feet. The wider stance allows for the hips and legs to turn and provides greater stability for the full swing.

Ball position can vary from club to club. As the clubs become longer, the ball is moved forward in the stance. For the five-wood, the ball and the hands are placed in position A. For the wedge, the ball moves back to position B while the hands remain in Position A.

For the other clubs, the ball should be located between positions A and B. The ideal ball position varies for each player, and you will have to experiment to determine the best locations for yourself.

The differences in length of each club will influence your posture. The shorter clubs (wedge and nine-iron) will force you to bend over, while the five-wood and five-iron will require a more upright stance. Although the length of the club will alter your posture, the position of the hands relative to the left thigh should remain constant for all the clubs.

• *How do I swing?*

The swing begins with a deliberate takeaway that has the club moving in a straight path away from the ball and low to the ground for several inches. The takeaway is a slow, sweeping movement that is controlled by the left arm and shoulder.

At the first backswing checkpoint, the club toe points up and the shaft is parallel to the target line. The backside of the left hand faces out and is also parallel to the target. The backswing continues until the hands reach shoulder height. As the body turns, the left shoulder comes under the chin. At the top of the backswing, the

Full swing with an iron

weight is transferred to the inside of the right leg and foot. The shoulders and arms initiate the beginning of the forward swing. The body uncurls as a reflexive response to being wound up like a top. During the forward swing, the weight is transferred from the right side to the left side. At ball impact, the clubface returns to its original position while the weight is approximately evenly distributed between both feet. At the conclusion of the swing the majority of the weight is on the left foot.

67

Practice Tips: When Do I Use Each Club?

A personal club log (see below) can help you learn when to use each club. When you practice at a driving range, record the average distance for each club. After a few weeks of recording your results, you will have a good idea of when to use each club.

Personal Club Log

Type of Shot	Club	Distance
Putt	Putter	_____
Chip	Wedge, nine-iron	_____
Pitch	Wedge, nine-iron	
Short iron	Seven-iron, eight-iron, nine-iron	_____
Middle iron	Four-iron, five-iron, six- iron	_____
Long fairway	Five-wood	_____
Tee shot	Five-wood	_____

During a round of golf let your mood and the playing conditions guide your club selection. Never force yourself to use a club that does not feel right. If you feel more comfortable with a five-iron than a five-wood, then use the five-iron. Another important point to remember is that most beginners seldom hit the ball over the green. They tend to overestimate their abilities and frequently hit shots short of the target. Always select enough club to get the ball to the target.

Full Swing ✔ List

Grip

❑ Place the hands one inch below the top of the club.
❑ Put the thumbs on the opposite sides of the grip.
❑ Use a baseball, interlocking, or overlapping grip.
❑ Maintain constant grip pressure.

Alignment

❑ Point the v's of both hands between the head and right shoulder.
❑ Aim the clubface toward the target.
❑ Align the shoulders, hips, and feet parallel to the target.

Stance

❑ Stand relaxed with the feet approximately shoulder-width apart.
❑ Position the ball between the front (ball position A) and the middle (ball position B) of stance.
❑ Place hands slightly ahead of the ball (hand position A).
❑ Bend at the hips, flex the knees, and place weight on the balls of the feet.
❑ Distribute weight evenly between the left and right side.

Swing

❑ Use a chin-to-shoulder swing (hands swung to shoulder-level).
❑ Use an arm-oriented swing with natural body movement.
❑ Transfer weight during swing.

Training Center

For this Training Center you will alternate shots using the different clubs.

Training Center

Equipment Needed
- *Five-wood*
- *Five-iron*
- *Seven-iron*
- *Nine-iron*

Task	Distance	Competence
❑ Hit golf ball with mini-swing using a tee	Any	3 for 3
❑ Hit golf ball with full swing using a tee	Any	3 for 3
❑ Hit golf ball airborne with mini-swing without a tee	Any	2 for 3
❑ Hit golf ball airborne with full swing without a tee	Any	2 for 3

Repair Shop

The most common swing errors are hitting the ball to the left (hook) or right (slice) of the target. When a golfer compensates for a hook or slice with homemade remedies, such as aiming in the opposite direction (for

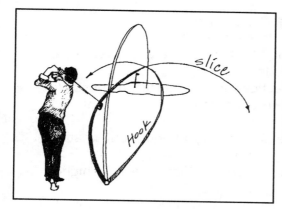

example, aiming more to the left for a slice), the problem worsens. The following are the Mechanic's treatments for chronic hookers and slicers.

Symptom: Hook.

Grip: Rotate the hands so the v's of both hands are pointing between your head and right shoulder.

Alignment: Use the "railroad" alignment drill to check the position of the club and body.

Stance: Move closer to the ball so that your hands are a few inches from your left thigh.

Swing: Swing the club down the line toward the target.

Symptom: Slice.

Grip: Rotate the hands so the v's of both hands point to between your head and right shoulder.

Alignment: Use the alignment drill to check the position of the club and body.

Stance: Move away from the ball so your hands are several inches in front of your left thigh.

Swing: Swing the club down the line toward the target.

The Golf Guy: How to Become a Lousy Golfer

For those of you tired of hearing, "This is what you should do," the following are suggestions for screwing-up.

- Set unrealistic goals, such as expecting to be a Tiger Woods within six weeks.
- Don't practice, and then wait for divine intervention from the Golf Gods.
- When you do practice, do it as quickly as possible.
- Compare your rate of improvement to that of others.
- When others are present, try to figure out what they are thinking about.
- Worry about whether your·golf score will be higher than your bowling average.
- Listen to the advice of anyone who owns a golf club and wears polyester.
- Be rigid and do not experiment with golf swing mechanics.
- Break a club when frustrated.

Ms. Etiquette: The Ten Golf Commandments

As you prepare for your first round of golf, Ms. Etiquette will review the Ten Commandments of Golf Etiquette.

I. I shall play by the rules of golf.
II. I shall dress like a golfer and not like a bowler.
III. I shall play as fast as possible.
IV. I shall not gamble, unless I can win.
V. I shall not drink and drive a golf cart.
VI. I shall repair any damage I cause to the golf course or friends.
VII. I shall not lie about my score, unless others have lied.

VIII. I shall not have pity parties, temper tantrums, or spaz attacks.

IX. I shall purchase copies of *KISSing Golf* for loved ones.

X. I shall have fun.

Reward

To reward yourself for completing the full swing lessons, and to prepare for your round of golf, treat yourself to a pair of golf shoes. Do golf shoes make a difference? Yes! The spikes on a golf shoe provide support and help improve your balance during the swing. Factors to consider are fit, cost, materials (waterproofed leather is preferred, but more expensive), and style.

Chapter Eight
Let's Go Golfing

*Golf is the most fun you can have with-
out taking your clothes off.*

—Chi Chi Rodriguez

Congratulations! You are now ready to play at a golf course.

Where Do I Play?

The first decision you must make is selecting which course to play. If your first golf experience is not just right, you may never go golfing again. The following are the key factors to consider when selecting a course to play.

• *Course Difficulty*

The most important course selection consideration is the difficultly level of the course. The ideal beginner course is a short course (6,000 yards or less) with few or no hazards, such as sand bunkers and water hazards. The type of course that usually meets those require-ments is often referred to as a "par three," "putt-and-pitch," or "executive" course.

• *Time*

A round of golf should take at most four hours to complete, but at crowded courses a round may take more than five hours to finish. If possible, you should try to avoid the prime golf times such as weekends and evenings.

• *Cost*

Golf is an expensive pastime. Greens fees for a public course may range from $10 to $150. Some courses inflate their fees by requiring golfers to rent a motorized golf cart.

• *Carry, Pull, or Ride?*

At the course you will select your mode of transportation. The choices are walking and carrying your clubs, walking with a pull cart, or riding in a motorized cart. For most beginners walking with a pull cart makes the most sense. A pull cart is inexpensive to rent ($2-$5) and will relieve you of the chore of carrying your bag. You will also gain the health benefits of walking.

• *Number of holes to play*

A regulation round of golf includes eighteen holes. Some courses allows golfers to play, and pay, for nine holes. I strongly recommended that you play only nine holes the first few times you go to a golf course.

• *Playing partners*

Although you do not have to golf with someone, some courses are so crowded that they require golfers to play in groups of four. For your first experience, it is best to play with someone with a lot of patience and understanding (that usually means someone other than your spouse).

What Do I Bring to the Course?

You will need additional equipment to play a round of golf. Although you are allowed to carry up to fourteen clubs, you can get by with less clubs. A basic starter set includes the following clubs: five-wood, five-iron, seven-iron, nine-iron, wedge, and putter.

You will also need a golf bag to carry the clubs. In addition to your clubs, the following items should be packed in your golf bag.

Bag ✔ *List*

❑ Clubs (no more than 14)
❑ Balls (10)
❑ Club towel
❑ Hand towel
❑ Tees (18)
❑ Ball mark repairer
❑ Shoes
❑ Bandages
❑ Glove hat
❑ Ball marker
❑ Water container
❑ Umbrella
❑ Munchies
❑ Rain gear
❑ Pencil

If you plan to carry your bag, then weight becomes an important consideration. A fully packed golf bag can weigh from thirty to sixty pounds. The weight can be reduced by eliminating infrequently used clubs, removing the head covers, and using a lightweight bag.

What Should I Do Before I Tee Off?

Here's a brief checklist of the things you need to do before you start playing:

Pre-Round ✔ List

❑ Pick up a score card and pencil from the clubhouse.

❑ Review the card (see the following section).

❑ Complete your golf stretches.

❑ Hit a few practice putts at the practice green.

❑ If time permits, hit a few balls at the driving range.

❑ Place a few balls and tees, a ball marker, and a ball mark repairer into your pockets.

❑ Lower your expectations.

❑ Go to the potty.

❑ Lower your expectations further.

Reading a Golf Card

A golf card contains a lot of valuable information. The following is a guide for deciphering a card.

• *Course layout*

The course layout is the map of the course. It identifies where each hole is located and the geographic features of each hole. Taking time to review the layout before you tee off will help you avoid getting lost on the course.

The eighteen holes will be divided into the "front nine" (holes #1-#9) and "back nine" (holes #10-#18). The topography of each individual hole will also be displayed. The fairway may be straight, doglegged (the hole bends to the right or left), uphill, or downhill. Although the actual placement of the hole may vary daily, the shape and contour of each green will be illustrated.

• *Hole yardage*

The score card identifies the distance from the various teeing areas to the center of the green for each hole. Some courses may have as many as three or four teeing areas for each hole, so the hole yardage will vary depending on teeing area used.

The teeing area furthest from the hole is usually designated as the "championship" tee and often identified with black tee markers. The "men's" teeing area is identified with white tee markers. The red markers are nearest to the hole and are designated as the "front" or "ladies'" tee.

• *Par and hole handicap/difficulty*

Each teeing area will have a corresponding par and handicap rating. The par score identifies the expected score on a given hole. The hole handicap indicates the general difficultly of that hole as compared to the other

78

COURSE RATING/SLOPE

Gold	70.1	120
Blue	68.3	117
White	65.5	108
Red	63.7	96

Hole	Men's Gold	Blue	White	Par	Hdcp			0 + −				Ladies' Hdcp	Red
1	458	425	385	4	3							3	217
2	171	155	133	3	13							13	99
3	493	482	450	5	7							7	376
4	363	338	295	4	9							9	224
5	151	139	125	3	17							17	102
6	342	325	291	4	11							11	234
7	338	313	274	4	15							15	231
8	437	397	373	4	5							5	268
9	453	422	383	4	1							1	268
Out	3206	2996	2709	35									2019
10	193	168	130	3	12							12	78
11	591	567	504	5	4							4	460
12	180	165	133	3	8							8	117
13	479	458	426	4	2							2	225
14	382	358	318	4	10							10	233
15	439	424	390	4	14							14	324
16	346	323	275	4	16							16	234
17	151	140	135	3	18							18	103
18	541	525	473	5	6							6	440
In	3302	3128	2784	35									2214
Out	3206	2996	2709	35									2019
Total	6508	6124	5493	70									4233

Handicap

Net Score

Scorer   Attest   Date

Shot Selector
(800) 878-9288

Score card

golf holes. The most difficult hole receives a handicap of one while the easiest hole receives a ranking of eighteen. The par score and the hole handicap may vary according to each teeing area.

• Course rating/slope

The overall course rating and slope reflects the general difficulty of the course. These are standardized scores that allows comparisons between courses. The course rating is the expected score of an expert golfer for a given course. The slope score is a general measure of difficultly that is used in the computation of a golfer's handicap. The higher the course rating and slope score, the greater the difficulty of the course. For example, a course with moderate playing difficulty will have a slope rating of approximately 115.

• Course rules

Most courses follow the United States Golf Association (U.S.G.A.) rules. Any additions or modifications to the U.S.G.A. rules are usually noted on the backside of the score card. Information concerning hazards, out-of-bounds, and course etiquette is also noted.

How Do I Record My Score?

The score for a given golf hole is the number of strokes required to get the ball from the teeing area to the hole. Because the expected score varies from hole to hole, golfers use terms that allow comparisons between holes. The following are the various scoring terms and their definitions.

• Par

A score that an expert golfer is expected to make for a given hole. There are three possible par scores:

three, four, and five. The par for a given hole is prede-termined by a variety of factors, such as distance and difficulty. In general, the shorter holes are par threes (220 yards or less) while the longer holes are par fives (500 yards or more). The majority of holes on a golf course (approximately twelve) are par fours.

• Birdie

A score that is one stroke under par for a given hole. For example, a two on a par three and a four on a par five are both considered birdies.

• Eagle

A score on a given hole that is two strokes under par. For example, a three on a par five is an eagle. Eagles are rare and most frequently occur on par fives.

• Bogey

A score that is one stroke above par. For example, a five on a par four is a bogey.

• Double Bogey

A score that is two strokes above par. A seven on a par five would be a double bogey.

• Triple Bogey

You got it. A score three strokes over par.

• Hole-in-one

The ultimate dream for a golfer is to complete a hole in one stroke. This extremely rare score will usually oc-cur on a par-three. A hole-in-one is also referred to as an ace. If you ever do achieve a hole-in-one, you will be the envy of your golfing partners and be assured of a special place in golf heaven.

81

The Typical Golf Hole

Let us walk through a typical hole to give you a feel for what to expect when you go golfing.

You first must locate the front teeing area identified by the red tee markers. The tee box is the only area where you can tee the ball up. You can tee the ball up anywhere between the tee markers and up to two club lengths behind the markers. While the ball must be hit from the designated area, you do not have to stand in the tee box. Before you hit the ball, review the card to identify where the target area, hazards, and the green are located. Unless the hole is very short, you will tee off with your five-wood.

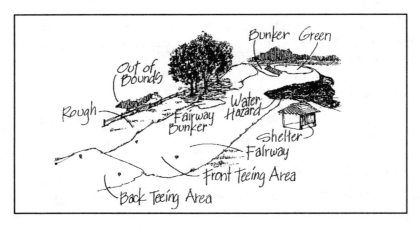

After you tee off, your ball will be in the fairway or rough. Although the rules of golf require you to play the ball as you find it, I recommend that beginners play by winter rules. Winter rules are sometimes allowed on a course that has impaired conditions, such as arid or soggy fairways, and allow the golfer to move the ball one-club length until a playable location is found. For your first few rounds of golf, I strongly suggest that you move the ball around so that you hit from a good lie. It should be noted that winter rules are not endorsed as

"rules" per se by the major golf organizations. The con-
cept was probably started by golfers trying to bend the
rules to improve their score.

The order of play is dictated by the distance of each
player's ball to the hole—the player furthest away from
the hole plays first. With the exception of the first hole,
the order of play from the tee area is determined by the
score on the previous hole. The player with the lowest
score on the previous hole earns the honors to tee off
first.

On most holes, except the short par threes, your
second shot will be with the five-wood. (Remember, that
you cannot tee the ball up in the fairway.) As you get
closer to the green, you must determine the distance
to the green and select the appropriate club. Most course
have yardage markers located throughout the fairways
to help you compute this distance.

Should I Keep Score?

The rules of golf require that you record each attempted shot, including the swing and miss, as a stroke.
The beginner's total score for a round of golf can be
embarrassingly high. If you do not keep a record of your
score, you will have no way to gauge your rate of improvement.

One strategy is not to worry about your bad scores
and only keep a record of your best scores. Is that dis-
torting the truth? Sure, but why deal with reality when
you don't have to? After several rounds you can start
paying attention to your total score, acquire a handicap,
and have a reality check.

A handicap is the numbers of strokes over par you
average over several rounds of golf. For example, a
twenty handicap indicates that on the average you score
a ninety-two on a par seventy-two course. The handicap
is also a standard score that can be adjusted for the
difficulty level of different courses. The easiest way to

establish a handicap is to keep a record of your scores and pay your local course a small fee to compute your handicap.

The Golf Guy: Minister Rules

One of my playing partners is a Baptist pastor who is a mediocre player yet has more fun playing golf than anyone I know. How can someone who has limited skills love the game so much? It's because he plays by "minister rules." For example, when the pastor hits a bad shot he believes that a higher authority allows for the shot to be replayed without any penalty (often referred to as a "mulligan"). The minister also doesn't have to make any short putts because God believes in gimmies.

Golf purists would point out that minister rules violate the basic tenets of the game. It is very important to understand and play by the official rules of golf. Yet, the Golf Guy firmly believes we should not forget that the purpose of golf, or any game, is to have fun. If playing by minister rules makes golf more enjoyable for you, then do it. The Golf Guy realizes that he may be delivered to golf purgatory for encouraging you to bend the rules, but go ahead and give yourself that putt.

Ms. Etiquette: What if...

The following are some of the questions that might arise during your golfing adventure. Many of the answers provided below are influenced by the rules of the game. In keeping with the *KISSing Golf* philosophy, Ms. Etiquette will briefly address only the most common questions. Otherwise, you would be overwhelmed with information. As your game improves, you

84

can refer to *The Rules of Golf* for all the possible options.

•What if it starts to rain?

Golf can be played in a variety of weather conditions. Unless the conditions are unbearable, play should continue.

•What if there is a lightning or thunder storm?

Although the odds of being struck by lightning are low, the annual death rate of golfers hit during storms illustrates the need for special precautions. At the first indication of lightning, you should immediately halt play and seek shelter. Each course should provide you with shelter information. The key thing to remember is to get to shelter as quickly as possible.

•What if I lose my ball?

Golfers become very possessive of their golf balls. As many golfers have said, "I'm staying here until I find that damn ball." In fact, many golfers carry a ball retriever so they can recover balls hit into water hazards.

The rules of golf allow you five minutes to look for a lost ball. If there is a group behind you, then you should play another ball or let the group play through. If you cannot find the ball, the penalty is loss of a stroke and distance—you must return to the original point of play and replay the shot. All golfers lose golf balls and you need to get use to it.

When you hunt for a lost ball, you may find orphaned balls. Before you thank the golf gods for replacing your lost ball, you must make sure the ball does not belong to another player. To prevent the mistake of playing the wrong ball, you should write an identifying mark on all your balls.

• *What if I have to hit the ball over water?*

When confronted with a water hazard, most beginners experience Loch Ness syndrome and assume their balls will be gobbled up by the water monster. If you do hit the ball into the water, the rules of golf require you to take a one stroke penalty and drop the ball nearest the point it crossed the water hazard. The ball can be recovered from the hazard, but the penalty is still enforced.

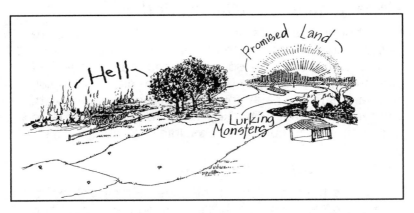

Ms. Etiquette's suggestion is to try to hit the ball over the hazard once or twice. If you are unable to hit the ball over the water, then place the ball on the opposite side of the water hazard. Although this suggestion violates the rules, you will be able to avoid the horrible monster.

• *What if I hit the ball out of bounds?*

Courses often designate certain areas as "out of bounds." These areas are usually clearly marked (white stakes or lines) or described on the score card. The penalty for hitting a ball out of bounds is loss of distance and stroke—you must replay the shot from the original spot and take a one-stroke penalty. Even if you recover your ball, the penalty is still enforced. As this is one of golf's most severe penalties, the advice is simple—don't hit the ball out of bounds.

• *What if I am playing slowly?*

As mentioned before, the required etiquette when playing slowly is to allow faster groups to play through. That means standing aside on a hole and letting the group behind you hit and move ahead of your group. In addition to letting others play through, you can speed up your rate of play by completing your shot preparation as your playing partners are hitting. You should decide on the type of shot to be played, select the proper club, and take any practice swings while your partners are playing (remember not to disturb your partners while they address and hit their shot). The time between the previous shot and your shot should be less than a minute. By quickly completing your pre-shot preparation, you will avoid being busted by the the golf rangers.

• *What if I hit the ball toward someone?*
Yell, "Fore."

• *What if I hear someone yell, "Fore?"*
Duck.

• *What if I get frustrated?*
Hey, that's golf.

Reward: The Big One

Can you guess the final reward? You are right! It is a set of golf clubs. Is it mandatory to buy a set of clubs to continue with the game? No! However, a set of your own clubs might help improve your commitment to the game and your score.

If you purchase a set of clubs, you will need to consider the following questions.

• How much does a set of clubs cost?

The cost of the clubs is the first, and most important, consideration in selecting a set of clubs. A new set of clubs can range from $150 to more than $1000. A used set of clubs may be purchased for less than $100.

• What types of clubs should I buy?

The type of clubs is not as important as the fit of the clubs. Before you spend money on clubs, you should be properly fitted. The clubs must match your physical features, swing characteristics, and personal preferences. I strongly recommend that you contact a golf professional or experienced club maker for information concerning proper fit. After you learn the basics of club fitting you can then shop around for the best deal.

Closing Thoughts

The real challenge of golf is to have fun. To achieve that goal you must shift from a thinking mode to an experiential mode. During a round of golf you must let your skills naturally surface. When you finish your round, measure your performance not by your score, but by how much fun you had.

Chapter Nine
What's Next?

*Golf: The most damn fun anybody
ever had.*

—Cy Manier

Congratulations on your round of golf! I hope that
the experience was enjoyable for you. The following questions will help you decide whether you want to continue
learning how to golf.

1) Did you have fun?

2) Do you have the time and patience to continue with
   learning how to golf?

3) Are there people in your life with whom you would
   enjoy playing golf?

If you answered yes to the above questions, then
golf may be for you.

Selecting a Golf Professional

KISSing Golf has served as your introduction to golf.
To graduate to the next skill level you must go beyond
the lessons in this book. Although the avenues open to
you are many, taking lessons from a golf professional is
the most efficient way to improve your golfing skills.

There are two types of lessons offered by golf professionals. An individual golf lesson is a one-on-one lesson that usually lasts from thirty minutes to one hour. Individual lessons can be expensive ($20 or more per lesson), but provide extensive personalized instruction and feedback. Lessons are also offered in a group format with one instructor for two or more golfers. The group lessons are considerably less expensive, but may lack the concentrated instruction of an individual lesson.

There are several considerations in selecting a golf professional. Make sure the individual is an accredited instructor. For golf professionals, the primary training and certification organization is the Professional Golf Association (P.G.A.). Consider the type of lesson you desire and the cost of the lesson, and then determine if you like the instructor and that you are comfortable taking criticism from this person.

Other Ways to Improve

If the self-instructional approach that characterized this book met your needs, then you might want to create your own instructional library. There are hundreds of golf videotapes, books, and training devices, but before you purchase any of the instructional materials, I suggest that you try to obtain the books or videotapes for reviewing through a public library or video shop.

Closing Thoughts

It has been my pleasure to serve as your guide to the world of golf. I hope that through *KiSSing Golf* you have caught the golfing bug. Golf is one of the few sports that you can grow into (as illustrated by Bob Hope and other octogenarians) and can also be enjoyed by couples. If you continue playing golf, please keep in mind the two fundamental principles of this book—have fun and always keep it simple. May the golf gods be with you.